PRELIMINARY REPORT

JON DAVIS

PRELIMINARY REPORT

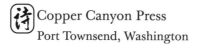 Copper Canyon Press
Port Townsend, Washington

Cover art: Grant Hayunga, *Autumn Sky at Dusk,* 2002. Mixed media, 48 × 48 inches.

Copper Canyon Press is in residence at Fort Worden State Park in Port Townsend, Washington, under the auspices of Centrum. Centrum is a gathering place for artists and creative thinkers from around the world, students of all ages and backgrounds, and audiences seeking extraordinary cultural enrichment.

LIBRARY OF CONGRESS CATALOGING-IN-PUBLICATION DATA
Davis, Jon, 1952–
Preliminary report / Jon Davis.
   p.   cm.
ISBN 978-1-55659-315-4 (pbk.: alk. paper)
I. Title.
PS3554.A934912P74 2010
811′.54 — dc22

2010004653

9 8 7 6 5 4 3 2 FIRST PRINTING

COPPER CANYON PRESS
Post Office Box 271
Port Townsend, Washington 98368
www.coppercanyonpress.org

ACKNOWLEDGMENTS

I thank the editors of the following journals for publishing these poems:

American Letters & Commentary: "Notes to *The Haitian Poems* of Madeleine du Plessix"

Calapooya: "Bouquet," "Jade Buddha"

Chokecherries: "The Good Life"

Colorado Review: "Art & Life," "A Modern Form"

Dragonfire: "Black Spaniel & Drunk Parents," "Festival of Natural Disasters," "Invention of Memory"

Exquisite Corpse: "An Introduction to Tonight's Performance"

Frank: "Hunger Song," "Ma Roulotte"

The Iowa Review: "Giraffe," section 3 of "Midlife Suite" as "Neck"

Mid-Atlantic Review: "A Brief History of Heartbreak," "The Fish," "Piñon & Moon"

Narrative: "In Darkness," "Portrait of My Mother, 1957," "What Now?," "Yodel"

New Mexico Poetry Review: "Moon, Predawn Courtyard, Santa Fe, New Mexico"

Ontario Review: "Loving Horses"

Oregon Literary Review: "The Fish," "Horse in Shadow," "Utilitarianism"

Ploughshares: "The Accounting," "The Horse, Susan Said," "What Is a Person? What Must One Do?"

The Salt Journal: "The Pot Spinners"

Sentence: "Accident," "Etymology," "The Memorist"

Sin Fronteras/Writers Without Borders: "Tuba City"

"Bouquet," "Horse in Shadow," "The Horse, Susan Said," and "Loving Horses" appeared in *Cadence of Hooves: A Celebration of Horses* (Yarroway Mountain Press, 2008).

"The Incandescence of the Present" and "The Sea. Not the Sea." appeared in *Local Color* (Palanquin Press, 1995).

"The Accounting," "Art & Life," "Jade Buddha," "The Horse, Susan Said," "Midlife Suite," "A Modern Form," "Piñon & Moon," and "What Is a Person? What Must One Do?" appeared in *Photographers, Writers, and the American Scene: Visions of Passage* (Arena Editions, 2001).

"Horse in Shadow" and "Loving Horses" appeared in *Poets of the American West* (Many Voices Press, 2010).

"The Modern Condition" appeared in *Sixty Years of American Poetry* (Harry N. Abrams, Inc., 1996).

"The Accounting" appeared in *Strange Attractors: Poems of Love and Mathematics* (A K Peters, Ltd., 2008).

"Preliminary Report from the Committee on Appropriate Postures for the Suffering" appeared in the *2009 Poetry Calendar* (Alhambra Publishing, Belgium, 2008).

"Loving Horses" appeared in the *2010 Poetry Calendar* (Alhambra Publishing, Belgium, 2009).

Thanks to Lannan Foundation for a 1998 Literary Award, to the National Endowment for the Arts for a 2005 Literature Fellowship, and to the Institute of American Indian Arts for a spring 2006 sabbatical that allowed me to complete this book.

Thanks to Greg Glazner, Arthur Sze, Dana Levin, Dick Allen, and Santee Frazier for their close reading, support, and friendship, and for their own poems, which continue to serve as models and measures. And thanks, always, to Teresa.

for Teresa
    for Grayce
        for Gregory, Briana & Matthew

CONTENTS

II

III

PRELIMINARY REPORT

dennoch preisen

RILKE

A chattering in the eaves. A forceful muttering.
Words carefully chosen, then smeared with beargrease.
Not the language of flurry and ease. Not the song
of the defrocked vigilante. Not the hemmed and attenuated.
The truculent minnesinger. But the harried flight
of the marauding crow. Missile sprung from the desert.
Catapulted vixen. Acrid linguist. Cartwheeling Taoist.
It's rumored they could fly, watch you eating your rice —
your ineffectual chopsticking and long-grained beard —
hover above you, disembodied, then return before dawn.
That they were not given to gossip was a godsend.
But what about this sputtering saxophone? How to explain that
to the moderate drinkers gathered seatward this evening?
Ladies and gentlemen, the modern attention requires
disjunctiveness, ballistics, contortions. Requires
that we drive this tractor-trailer filled with tortured geese
through the Holland Tunnels of your ears. Forgive us,
we can neither fly nor cartwheel effectively. Therefore
we have chosen the screams of wounded animals as our theme.
That there will be more wounded requiring more such
compositions is a given. That ticket prices will reflect this trend.
That you should use the exits positioned at the foot of the stage
and not burst unannounced through the corrugated steel.
The management would like to remind you that one *hails*
a taxi, one does not *ambush, derail,* or otherwise *interfere with*
or *impede* such commuter-oriented vehicles. They are a
privilege and not a right. If the perpetrator does not
come forward, we will remain in our seats until we have
exhausted the abuses we have planned for the various instruments.
That you might wish to avoid this. That if the severed hand
on the apron is any indication. That announcements from the stage

shall be random and without merit. That our purchase on reality
seems tenuous. Please welcome if you will. You may choose
not to welcome, of course, but the performance will occur regardless.

Moments blow through us like wind—

Curled leaves, swirl of dried grass, shape of a mother's face—

Parched leaves—

Carrying fear wearing the mark of secrecy—

A voice grown deeper—

Some said: The snake died trying to eat a too-large mouse—

Some said: There was a party, everyone drunk, and four days later, the snake
        under the sofa pillows, dead—

Some said: A vagueness fell like a veil over her face and she was never herself again—

Memory said: Precisely—

First you open your eyes and then the eyes inside your eyes open—

Memory, someone said, is a poor servant, a poorer master—

Memory of bombs detonating, shaking ground—

Memory of wild dogs in the fennel—

Memory of the movie that was really a novel that was really a dream—

All of it in you like shrapnel—

You cannot remember what he said but cannot forget how you felt when he
said it —

Something about his face — the angular glance, a fierceness drawing his mouth
tight like a bow —

So when your mother explained that he was talking to her, not you, it was
no help —

O Blessèd One — Sacred Buddha — Krishna — all is maya —

Maya in you like shrapnel —

My daddy used to yodel.
That's not all my daddy did.
He'd wear plaid shorts & guinea Ts.
Grim in his swimsuit,
he'd grip a Bud & wade
in the gloaming, glower
in the grief of it. *It* being
most everything — neighbor
hovering over his single rose,
moon in the lilacs, wheel-less
tricycle in the pachysandra,
lovely wife & mother
athwart the chaise lounge.
My daddy used to yodel.
Late nights in the alley
between this basement
& the next. Old lummox
with a Gibson, he'd strum
& pluck until red-flashing
lights, a radio's hiss & crackle
scuttled his heartfelt song.
This world don't cotton
to no yodeler. So grim
& grimmer now my daddy is,
knobknee deep in plaid
& Bud. His yodel
stuffed. His Gibson packed.
That lovely wife & mother
gone. Gone to glower
& grief & gloaming.

You want to remember this. *But why?* Your mother,
hospitalized for depression. The doctors recommending —
No, that's the adult version. In the child's version,
there's no mother, then there's a mother. She looked off,
into the distance. She must have looked off
into the distance as if there were something to find
there. That could explain it. That staring
off as if the secret — *You were going to say as if the secret*
could be found there, but that wouldn't be right. As if
the secret could remain secret there. As if the husk of a secret
could be seen blowing off, tumbling across the mundane
face of the mundane. Then rubber smells — smell
of the raft, the flippers and mask. Gritty sand
everywhere. Shingled cottage. Wooden fence. A porch.
Lattice around it like a skirt. A gate with a lock.
You were looking under there. You were four years old
and you pressed your face close to the lattice and looked in.
In another version, your father was in there. *But, of course*
he couldn't have been. The men — *there must have been men —*
would have been your uncles, maybe your grandfather.
What would have been, for you, a hopeful longing
for your father's presence would have been, for them, a fear.
You remember them unloading a car — things sliding,
things tossed in the sand — and then, because
they were men, after all, loading a car back up.
In the child's version, what mattered was the smell of rubber,
the lattice, the darkness under the porch, gritty sand,
waves and sun, and your mother, staring calmly off
while everything swirled and crashed and tumbled around her.

At some point the ocean became,
in your mind, the sound of playing cards
riffling the spokes of your Schwinn.
In 1960. Three years before
the Beatles would hatch from the kitchen radio.
Like Mothra's offspring. Like some
new element. Atomic weight greater than
or equal to. Approaching the kicked-over
eight that you were instructed to read as
"infinity." Infinity, where miniskirted girls
were calling you. Were "beckoning."
Infinity with its spending money.
With its mod fashions and snappy answers.
Pi figured to twelve places
on the plastic sliderule plucked
from your button-down pocket.
Hypotenuse. Radius.
Trifecta. Squalor. Every band
called the Cellar Dwellers. A joke
whose punch line sounded "dirty"
so you laughed. Some kind of Hawaiian theme
governing patio behavior. Plastic glasses
that seemed to be made of rattan. Above you,
the X-15, pushing through the sound barrier
like a finger through saran wrap. Down
here: plastic patio lights lashed to a sapling.
Don Ho. Fruit drinks. Barbecue.
Thumbprint in the space-time continuum.
Nasty gash. John Gunther and Jacques
Cousteau. Rachel Carson.

Here on the cusp of puberty,
the knife's edge of the New Frontier,
a black spaniel, frantic, his nose
wedged in an Old Fashioned glass.
Someone's mother chortling
in the above-ground, her kamikaze
children launching from the redwood deck
their can-openers, their ruthless cannonballs.

For a long time, nobody mentioned
the pale blue fish, the transparent
and somnolent fish that drifted,
        dreamlike,
among the high-rises. Nobody
mentioned how they drifted with children
in their bellies, or how the children
        pressed their hands
against the insides of the cloudlike
stomachs. Or how the looks
on the children's faces were querulous,
        not frightened as
the adults had hoped. Not
stoical. Nor grieving. Hundreds of feet
up and the children stretched as if
        waking in their beds.
Happy, happy in the lee of their
dreams. Happy, with their warm feet
and the blue of the sky
        everywhere.
Below, on the streets, in the alarmed
houses, the adults began shouting
and pointing. Already, in earnest,
        the rescue had begun.

At nineteen I wanted to pierce the skin of the world's complacency.

I wanted to remind, for instance, my mother's uncle who slept on the couch
in his painter's coveralls & flannel shirt,

snoring so loudly we heard him in our upstairs bedroom,

that we are all slipping easily & precipitously toward death.

Because I was nineteen & had heard Janis howl,

heard Jimi slipping the guitar's needles under the skin of the world,

heard him conjure a panic of fiery spears that he hurled into the Woodstock sky.

Because that's what you do when you're nineteen.

You think you have the miserable secret to everything
& you're going to ruin the party,
hold the dead kitten by the tail & wave it in everyone's face.

But the party would ruin itself soon enough

And nothing would save you —
not the ducks nuzzling the corn mash in your hand,

not the peaceable kingdom of warblers that fluttered & flitted

that spring before the darkness yawned, tired of waiting, & began swallowing
everything you cared about —

Because maybe nothing is merely personal —
not the ducks nuzzling your hand for the mash

not your mother under the covers giggling with the family friend
who'd just slipped out of your younger brother's bed

not your father who parked in the driveway, his breathing more
like a flurry of gasps as he circled his hand
over the cancer that would kill him six months later.

Maybe the personal is always an expression of the cultural —

your father's cancer the world's cancer,

your mother's giggling the world laughing, saying *I had no idea & so what?*

& those ducklings — those clumsy balls of yellow down?

They were the world's clowns — the goofy mechanisms of their heads & bills,
the thoroughness with which they prodded each fold & edge, sliding

& nudging their blunt bills into the cracks between each finger
until just a few yellow grains were left

& you opened your hand & shook them free.

The dead kitten was a white Persian, blue-eyed, tail straight up as it strutted —
    somehow crushed under the loose cinderblocks piled by the back door.

And the great-uncle? He'd park his '58 Buick under the maple & doze &
    smoke while we played drinking games & setback inside my
    grandmother's house.

Sometimes he'd bring home an eel, curl it in a frying pan, sauté it in butter &
    eat it alone.

We never asked him who he was or how he came to sit at his sister-in-law's table.

We were probably passing a pipe or dealing a hand of setback when he died.

Who did we think we were, reading Kerouac & blasting *Exile on Main Street*

as if they were the loose wires of the world hissing and sparking?

As if we had only to walk out the front door & keep walking long enough

& we'd find a meaningful world out there among the microbuses & head shops,

among the posters, pipes & papers, the mud & litter of festivals,

nights spent circling the Green or standing under the flickering elms with
    Ripple wine in our paper bags?

Until one night, huddled at the top of the stairs,

listening to the Beatles' White Album burst from the speakers on *The Scene of
    the Unheard* at two in the morning,

the blue lights of the stereo glowing,

some scavenged Hendrix poster by Peter Max glowing in the black light,

it seemed we could feel the weight of moonlight falling on our shoulders

& we thought we were almost touching something real.

More real than the great-uncle on the couch.

More real than the shell-shocked father and his steady deathward plod.

More real than our mother's willed obliviousness.

We knew there were messages inside the messages inside the messages

inside the music and they had chosen us to tell themselves to.

But what were they saying? And what would we do if we knew?

For the lucky, it's years spent
spinning the frantic wheel
of a carnival bumper car,

lights swirling, the buzzing
and rumbling, sparking
and zapping, intent only

on causing the surprising
crash, the ram and counterram,
spun wheel, sudden surge

in reverse, the steady stare-down,
head-jerk, one car after
another until you find yourself

targeting the bare legs
of the college kid, his back
turned to unstick a clot

of stuck cars, bearing down,
full speed now, the humming
in your head now, until

the power dies and you stop
dead at his sneakered feet
and smile primly up —

— traffic's flamboyance a man pissing beside the entrance ramp
a modern form not unlike more ancient forms
here's where memory
where waves of light washed over him
where captious drivers honked and cursed
America encrypted there encoded
along the freeway banners flown by food items
along the ramps and bypasses pedestrians were turning radio
waves into the skeletal music we were known for
scrim of guitar a clatter a stomping
the plaintive singer floating above the audience
so sad and entertaining so virtual
and the stars burned magnificent in their boredom
and the cantillated hillsides
and the flaming montage we had long wanted to become
out there among the night's abstractions
among the panels the booths where the intrinsic clung to the honed
out there where the inputs were manifest
where the encryptions erupted and the blue
sparking where the eyes were
the blue sparking where we reached for each other
where two strangers held each other because —

The city will not speak
of that lost time. It is,
like a woman in shadow, entranced
and entrancing. Not lover. Not
friend. Not lifetime companion.
Flame in a glass. A moment
with the fragrance of wind
on its petals and stem. The blue wind,
which is the flower and the shadow also.
The flutterings between. The line
of light in the once clear lost
intimacy beyond the surface of things.
By turns, the gone moments shriek
and whisper. *Her hand
on my thigh.* City where the past
waits. Where it flops on its side
and purrs. Past with its shadows,
with its gulls and pelicans, each boat
drifting for real, for real like the rain
the city provides. If I were to dream
now, I would dream of flying. Not
as a child flies—a gliding, a gentle
flapping—but as an adult flies:
willful, encumbered. An arduous flight.
Almost waking in fear that I will not fly.
And in the end, the awful manipulation
of arms to fly nowhere near
the city of the past with its
incongruous, glorious monument
to One Life. When I rise tonight

among the blocks of shadow, I won't feel
a cool mist huffing off the bay. I won't
witness that strange landlocked
schooner, the heart. Maybe I will flicker
like those lights: *rain, bay,*
ship under sail. Maybe if I carried this
cup of sadness through the dusk-infused
cobblestone streets? Maybe
if I entered the body
still wandering that city — bay glittering,
boats knocking in their slips,
some circle broken, divided evenly into
thirds — *never* and *always* and *mouthful of dust?*
Maybe if I chose the city of moments?
Would I touch the glass? Would the glass
fog and a door slam against a cold
and a wind-tossed rain? I sing to hear
the words fall across the notes. Concrete —
the city — and steel. The simple lights
in windows, lace curtains, night stars numerous
and brilliant and the standing under alone.

Cold, the wind that riffs through the west-end door
sounding its low moan, grieving the moment's passing.
And cold the nose of the near-black gelding
where he stomps once in the glistening darkness,
the gentled night. My twelve-year-old daughter,
stiff in her jodhpurs and boots, removes one glove
and reaches a carrot toward the shadowed head.
"Good boy," she purrs. "Good boy." *Good boy,*
who'd bucked and lurched, galloping hell-bent
at the corrugated wall, whirling until he'd launched her
from the saddle into the dust-dazzled air.
"Good boy," she says. And he *is* — furious teacher,
unendurable bliss — because she *says* he is, loyal girl,
good friend, forgiver, profferer of carrots, wielder
of whips, tiny commander in her wafer-thin saddle.

Shadows below, not
of the insect itself

but of light's habitations,
the dimpled surface.

Movements abstracted
& mapped

on the stream bottom.
Parole et langue —

the structure of consciousness,
but even mind is turned

on the lathe of circumstance:
The water strider

always already adrift;
the streambed always already

expecting these circles
of light & shadow.

And we are not water striders,
though we skim our days,

though we navigate
the willow-lined shallows,

though we are steadfast
rowing lightly

on legs of language:
The shadows we cast

are insufficient
& mark our passage here.

WHAT IS A PERSON? WHAT MUST ONE DO?

In the midst of a life, out by the propane tank, by the stacked timbers,
while magpies keep up their quizzical catlike calls in the piñons—
a little threatening, their small part in the large thinking of the planet,
their part to be clever and quick, seasonal marauders at the dog dish—
the man drifts, sentenceless, and weary of dawn-light crisping
the east, weary of the nameless duskiness that lies on the pasture,
cozening the cattle, those great breathings, those stumblings at arroyo's edge,
weary of the dog on his morning route, sniffing each passing-in-the-night,
weary of his own failures—failures where the noun ratchets the world
into the paragraph, where the verb carries its incomplete instructions,
its vague commands, where the adjective grooms the unruly nouns.
What is a person? What must we do on our brief-hike-in-the-forest,
our crepuscular jig, our cash-starved vacation in the islands?

Coons in the trashbin, a clatter on the roof.

He wrote the word ART one hundred times, blindfolded, tried to erase it after
each writing.

It was either music or someone breaking a guitar.

It was either an amateur practicing scales or an experienced guitarist playing
with thick gloves.

Technique administered to a field of nonsense.

Light spoiling everything.

The autistic boy stood with his head in the piano case, feeling the overtones
like beach waves washing over his face.

Cannulated now. Intercessions everywhere now.

Bird told the television host, "I don't talk. I just want to play 'How High
the Moon.'"

Adumbrated, because we had a word for it.

In the polite introduction, in the splash of the detuned string.

Harmonics flung into silence or silence welcoming the harmonics.

The pleasures of art. The dangers.

He wanted to play *wash-of-dawn-light-through-a-vault-of-branches.*

He wanted to play *man-stumbling-through-a-dark-house.*

He wanted to play *sunlight-on-river-rocks.*

Instead he played *loose-electrical-wire-in-the-aftermath-of-a-hurricane.*

Snaking and hissing and sparking as refugees hurried past.

The belongings all over them, the burdens.

A ninety-year-old woman on a roof, the waters rising.

Numbers scraping their heels all night in the attic above them.

The accounting was necessary but brought them near death.

Like a fountain emptying itself for the tourists.

Couldn't the woman in the restaurant in the booth in the semiprivate room
    open her shirt?

In one view the numbers represented his errors of judgment.

In another, less sanguine view, his urge not to die into the dailiness.

The dailiness with its postponements, its sacks and surcharges, its relentless
    taxation.

Couldn't the woman lean against the bed's metal rails?

The punishment was merely a distraction from the real punishment, which was
    distraction.

Couldn't the woman suddenly before the meal was complete?

Couldn't she kiss him press him against the kitchen counter?

You can see how the notes trouble him, his lean

body angular with wanting, lost in the reckless now,

then *a glimpse a meaning a way in* fills him

& he *pounces*—you couldn't call it *playing,*

hands moved by gravity & obeisance, retooling

the whole chorus with odd splayed-finger assaults,

as if the piano were being rolled down

a city street & he, a curious passerby,

hunched now, chopping sideways at the keys,

were trying to kill music so the music could live.

PRELIMINARY REPORT FROM THE COMMITTEE ON
APPROPRIATE POSTURES FOR THE SUFFERING

We who wear clean socks and shoes are tired
of your barefoot complaining, your dusty footprints
on our just-cleaned rugs. Tired, too, of your endless ploys—
the feigned amputations, the imaginary children
you huddle with outside the malls, your rags and bottles,
the inconvenient positions you assume. Though we remain
impressed by your emaciation and your hunger and,
frankly, find you photogenic and think your images
both alarming and aesthetically pleasing, to do anything
more than sigh will require a complex process
of application and review, a process that is currently
in the development stage. Meanwhile, may we suggest
you moderate your public suffering at least
until the Committee on Appropriate Postures for the Suffering
is able to produce guidelines. Do not be alarmed.
The committee has asked me to assure you
that they are sensitive both to the aesthetic qualities
of your suffering—the blank stares, the neotenous beauty
as the flesh recedes and the eyes seem to grow larger,
the halos of flies—and to the physical limitations
of human endurance and the positioning of limbs.
They will, I am certain, ask that you not lift
your naked children like offerings to the gods.
On this topic, discussion has centered around the unfair
advantage such ploys give the parents of such children.
The childless, whether by choice or fate, are left
to wither silently in the doorways while those with children
proffer and gesticulate in the avenues unabated.

This offends our cherished sense of fairness,
the democratic impulse that informs and energizes
our discussions. Therefore, we ask for restraint,
and where restraint is lacking, we will legislate.
Please be forewarned. In addition, the committee
will recommend that the shouting of slogans,
whether directed at governments or deities, be kept
to a minimum. Not only is such shouting displeasing
aesthetically, but it suggests there is something
to be done. Believe me, no one is more acutely aware
of your condition than we who must ignore it every day
on our way to the capitol. In this matter, we ask only
that you become more aware of your fellow citizens,
who must juggle iPods, BlackBerries, briefcases
and cell phones, lattes. Who must march steadily
or be trampled by the similarly burdened citizens
immediately behind them. Your shouting and pointing
does not serve you well. Those of us employed
by the agency are sworn to oversee you. If we seem,
as you suggest, to have *overlooked* you instead,
that is an oversight and will be addressed, I am certain,
in our annual review. Please be aware: To eliminate
your poverty, your hunger, your aesthetically
pleasing, yet disturbing, presence in our doorways,
above our heating grates, in our subway tunnels,
and under our freeways would mean the elimination
of the agency itself and quite possibly a decline
in tourism. Those of us employed by the agency
have neither the stamina, persistence, nor the luminous
skin tones that you present to the viewing public.
Finally, to those who would recommend programs,
who would call for funding and action,
I must remind you that we have been charged not
with *eliminating* your suffering but with *managing* it.

II

Find yourself some good honest work. That's what my mama said. Find some good honest work. Do it for eight hours. Come home, eat some pasta, drink a glass of vino, put your feet up. When it comes to footwear—don't skimp. Buy good shoes with thick soles. Rubber soles, not leather. Leather will make you slip and slide. Let the pimps wear the leather soles. You get a good, solid shoe. A black shoe with a thick rubber sole. A low heel. With laces. A slip-on is a slip-off. Don't take chances. Get good honest work. Buy good shoes and a stiff mattress. No feather beds for a working man. A hardworking man needs a hard mattress. None of these water beds, either, she said. You'll dream of the sea, and a man dreaming of the sea is a dangerous man. Find yourself a woman with good legs and hips. A woman who can carry children and make a spicy sauce. Don't marry a thin woman—she'll move too fast and be restless in bed. She'll keep a working man awake and love shopping too much. Find a woman who can grow pole beans. A woman who can lose herself in the good dirt, who can stake the tomatoes and knows how much basil makes a handful. Some women's hands can't hold a handful of basil—there's too much space between their fingers. Don't marry a woman with too much space between her fingers. That's what my mama said. Buy good shoes and a stiff mattress. Find a woman with good hips and strong legs. Keep the kids in the yard. Don't let them wander. Get a small dog with a big bark. Chain him out by the garden. You can't be too careful. Go to church every Sunday. Confess your sins. Make a good Communion. Bring a plate of something sweet to the St. Anthony's bake sale. Keep the kids clean and out of the dirt. And don't let them run with the Dolcini girls. For God's sake, she said, don't let them run with those *skinny* Dolcini girls.

Desktop. Desk drawer. Plastic mat. Because he could forget nothing. Because he could not find his way to the story. Because this detail was equal to that and nothing suggested a linear sequence. Because the fuse did not lead to the bomb and the bomb did not explode. Because when it was night it was all night and when it was day it was thoroughly day, and when the dawn came it was dawn and in the dusk, all was dusk. Because when he scratched his head the scratching had the heft of a novel. And when he glanced in the mirror, he saw the death of his father. And the death of his father was just some hay tossed to the meandering cattle. *Three nickels, two dimes, and a penny. A guitar tuner. Two Bose speakers. The rush of the computer fan. The ticking of the keyboard. The computer screen reflected in the window. The light from the screen glinting on his glasses. A Borders receipt. A bottle of water. A cup of coffee suddenly in his hand.* He was reading a book called *Being Good.* He was near finishing. Then he could begin again. Each event led only to its repetition. First the sun, then the moon, then the sun again. Someone knocked. Someone entered. It was always the same person. Brighter now, his face. Shadowed by memory, but memory of what? Once he had killed his brother, he understood he would always be killing his brother. *Desk lamp. Sore elbow. Music from another room. Thin music from another room.* The alarm pulses from the bookshelves. *Three nickels, two dimes, a penny. A list of names and phone numbers. Passwords. Screen names. Fees and receipts.* He bought the motorcycle. The motorcycle had an accident inside it. You couldn't tell. Not at first. The fuse did not lead to the bomb and the bomb did not explode. He was born and the stars decided. Rope around his neck, he sat on the tree branch. Practicing. Rehearsing. There was death in the motorcycle and he would ride it. *Binoculars. CD. Violence of the white page.* The accident was not an accident. The accident was a time, a moment, an intersection. Not caused. *Black pen. Bank statement. Desk calendar.* The accident was a thing, an item in a list. Not done. Then done. Checked off. Already checked off. Not completed, but done. *Spring binder. Stapler. Paperweight. Fan.*

Uncertainty was in the syllables, was tied to each letter like a plastic flag. Like the flags the one-legged surveyor instructed his assistant to tie along the edges of our property. Our property, which existed as a plat, as a map in a file. A file thc birds inhabited as random pencil-marks, as coffee stains. A file filled with longing as words are filled with a longing to be things. As the dung beetle larvae must be filled with a longing to be language — that afterlife, that surplus value. *Words add to the senses,* but to what do the senses add? Once, in the haze of some over-the-counter remedy, I thought or dreamed or heard the finches' chatter outside my window evolving into a language. Not English exactly, but an imprecise song which said, or seemed to say, *We wake up hungry. We go to sleep hungry. And hunger is what we dream.* Over and over they sang from the juniper by the window. Even past midnight they'd wake from where they'd perched as if filed in a drawer and repeat their two-syllable call: *hun-ger, hun-ger.* And hadn't I waded farther into the river's chilling waters? Hadn't I sought sustenance in the too-cold dawn, walking the ridgeline underdressed, crawling under wild rose and penstemon to see the yellow bird singing from the low branches of the piñon? Hadn't I hungered to know its name? And hadn't its name called the bird closer? That fluttering shiver, that song distributed along the light-slick branch, that birdless name, scraps of it clinging to the needles, that name with round black eyes, querulous, calling me into the presence of clouds, slight breeze shearing across my cheek and hair, rough branch pressing my shoulder, rough gravity tugging me earthward, and all of it — bird and birdsong, brush and branch, ridgeline, property, hunger — all of it sliding now (in language) toward the sun.

What we need, Susan said, shifting in the rattan chair so the entire chair winced, *is to live in such a way that we don't need art.* She was holding a glass of white wine in her right hand, touching her right wrist lightly with her left fingertips. She was leaning forward out of the porch light that must have been shining into her eyes when she sat up, obliterating the rest of us. *So art,* someone asked — it must have been James, whose idealism was somehow unshaken by his endless close reading of Nietzsche — *is a luxury, or worse, its abundance a measure of our inadequacies?* Susan leaned back and let the light mottle her thin face. When she swirled her wine, the light flashed in the maples above us. *If we lived well,* she ventured, *we wouldn't need Van Gogh or Mozart or Bird. There wouldn't be anything left to transform into art. Just think of those cave paintings in Lascaux. It was scarcity made them paint. It was failure. Don't you think? If the hunt is always successful, there's no need to paint. But,* James said — he was clearly agitated by Susan's reasonableness — *wouldn't you miss those paintings? I'd miss them,* Susan said, *if I needed them. But I wouldn't need them. But here's the good news,* James said — you could tell by the rhythm of his words, the pacing, that this was his final statement — *the hunt will never be successful enough.* Susan smiled and swirled her wine, willing — it was "her way" and one reason we enjoyed her presence — to let James have the last word. What we didn't know until later, when we rehashed the discussion, was that we had all been thinking of Susan's ex-husband, a concert cellist whose endless march up and down both coasts, following whatever pittance was allowed a practitioner of his obscure but celebrated art, eventually became too much of a burden for Susan, who wanted both the romance of art and the stability of home and family. So James, afraid that their theoretical disagreement might turn personal, decided to let Susan have the last word, *thereby,* James would later say, clearly relishing the irony implicit in Susan's final silence, *acknowledging the poverty of our relationships and opening the way for art.*

A crown or the masts of a fishing boat. The sea, perhaps, or the disclosures and erasures by which the sea is known. The sea like the approach of a lover. A man on his back on the floor, a woman on the bed. Passing time like that. How the past manifests itself, blooms on the verge of sleep. Words like notes sung through a saxophone, soft-edged and thick with feeling, gestures toward open-ness, loneliness blowing its little riffs through the voices. Any two people could talk like this, but the price. They could take a knife and scrape it all down. They could cover the sea with white — white snow, white sand. Strange figures could whirl off the brush tip. Birds? Men? The surface transformed. A crown or a fishing boat's mast? A trident or a star? Still the sea beneath it all. Still the man calling to the woman. Still the woman calling to the man. Erasures, disclosures. The waves and the fishing. Not what we see of the fishing, but the fishing itself. The essential fishing. Not depicted and so uncorrupted by sight. The water touches the water touches the water. He gives her his damaged mother, his father suffer-ing the muted stovelight of the past, a morning when the lawn was frosted as the sea is frosted if it is the sea. They give each other a share in their suffering: the longing, the secret expressions of that, the loss the loss the loss. She gives him the dismal bookish nights of her adolescence, the boyfriends and the girls they left her for. The sea. Not the sea. The sea like the approach of a lover. The crown or the masts of a fishing boat. But more hopeful. Not undertaken or seen as undertaking. Not love as project, but as color, texture, a sea underlying the dutiful managings of surface. Disclosures and erasures and the thing that survives. Hidden and inexplicable and so imperturbable. Incorruptible. The water touches the water touches the water. The sea, perhaps. The disclosures and erasures by which the sea is known.

Tenable, from *tenēre,* to keep or to hold. The unholdable. Silence within words. Fish in the hand. When the hurricane struck, Uncle Dave drove us all to the beach. The sky was a dark lid, bolted down over the ocean. Wind lifted the water into waves. Walls of water, churning, crashing. Sizzling sand. When the tiny sharks called *dogfish* were left behind, we tried to grab them by their rough tails. They kept slipping away. The untenable. That which cannot be held. God of dogfish. Of warblers. Of water from a mountain spring. The words for those gods. *Tengo miedo.* I have fear. I hold it. Fear in a handful of dust. In the words for *handful-of-dust.*

André Breton thought what thought thought could lead us into the glittering kingdom of the real. If we paid attention. If we let it happen. If we stopped impish reason, with its calculators and moral imperatives. If we let the cantilevered mushrooms collude with the vapid Chernobyls of our celebrated ancestry, the real would limp, shyly and remorsefully, from behind the curtain, speaking with her actual, though unamplified, voice. André Breton, whose wife's hair was a brush fire, whose thought was summer lightning, whose etc. was an otter in the mouth of an etc. And the actual waiting for a cue. And the actual like a mouse among the table crackers.

And the cause of the accident was the woman's birth, her first steps on this wobbly planet. Her first-grade teacher scolding her so that she withdrew from the math problems, the blurred numbers scattering like centipedes across the paper, and later she became a writer of advertising, and therefore, after college, moved to Manhattan, bought a Lexus, and, when the past-deadline copy was finished, drove (the double yellow lines turning to centipedes in the just-before-sleep dream) off the road and through the newspaper stands lined alongside. The newspapers scattered, the weeklies and dailies, and the police report blamed her sleeping, but *she* knew, *she* knew—how each step, each decision, how each thought that thought thought had led her here, rain falling steadily on her shaking body, neck and back aching, hair tangled and soggy, the algebra turning into insects, the words glowing in their particularities, their unswerving allegiances, their habitats in their sentences, in their paragraphs. She knew, in the glare of the headlights, in the flash of red and blue, in the 3 a.m. bustle, in the grind and roar, in the honk and clatter, in the streaming and gloaming and never-ending of the gods' strange arrangements, she knew and, like André Breton, was delighted because she could not say she knew.

Greening now everywhere in the effervescent light. A shaking, a shimmering. O my lost world. Light carving a home in the grasses. A great absence under the unshadowed junipers. Wings stirring light. Tufts of thusness. Sprawling ontology. Fundament of blue in the mountains. A chasm, a gulf, an incipience when the earth tilts, opening itself to this clarity. Rabbit suddenly unsheltered on the llano. Owl arrowing low to safety. Jays and crows aloft now, bright fearless nouns now. Bright marauders in the kingdom of presence.

NOTES TO *THE HAITIAN POEMS* OF MADELEINE DU PLESSIX

1. Here, the language uncharacteristically suggests a world outside of language yet touched by language, as a boot might suggest a foot, as a night might discriminate a dawn. Contemporary thinkers, Madeleine du Plessix included, realize the futility in this proposition. No foot. No dawn. *Emptiness,* as the author stated in more than one of her "philosophical assays," *is its own petard.*

2. The cryptographical sense with which the author has imbued this passage is, of course, *sui generis,* and should be ignored at the reader's peril.

3. Translation: "She floats on language as water floats on a raft."

4. Though poorly rendered, the author intends here the international symbol meaning "crosswalk." (Scrawled marginalia: "this emblematic sign is a kind of attenuated language, neither oral, nor written — unsound[ed].")

5. Here, she claims to have "caught a tremendous fish." Roy Jones reports a certain skepticism among the guides at Harry's Bait Shack. (Autobiographical readings were anathema to the author, especially after her "Junk Bond Sequence" of the 1980s.)

6. This, authorities suggest, should be passed over in silence.

7. See note 6.

8. The oppressed in Haiti have a word for this phenomenon. Linguists believe the word is of West African origin, though little else is known.

9. The Russian aristocracy provided the model for this practice when they chose to speak in French. For the czars, the language's foreignness must have had, du Plessix believed, "both a lurid, depraved quality and a pleasing unintelligibility."

10. Should read "scared," not "sacred." (See uncorrected proofs and manuscripts collected at the Beineke Rare Book Library.)

11. "When the silken dragon was inflated and carried by the residents through the dirt streets," she noted in her journals, "the town took on a mythical quality that had not been present."

12. Text here is illegible. Originally thought to be a list of items the author planned to purchase and a note ("Bearded oysters. Menhaden. Paper bags. Steak. Arugula. Mayo. Visit quaint wooden church."), computer analysis suggests the following match: "Boarded windows. Men with paper bags sitting long-legged and lazy on the wooden porch—" Authorities cite photos that show a neighboring abandoned building much like the one described.

13. It was during this trip to Haiti that the author became enamored of what she called "her negritude." Biographers, citing her French/Irish ancestry, remain baffled by this statement.

14. Most scholars believe that *santería* rituals, including, perhaps, the accidental ingestion of the poisonous datura, were the "cause" of her feverishness. Others suggest she was spurned by a local fisherman, her bold advances taken instead as threats.

15. Her journal entry for July 13 of the same year: "Passionate lovemaking with Andre M. on beach south of the cottage."

16. Her attraction to the mysterious woman (some think the daughter of a Haitian sugarcane mogul) referred to only as S. would later create "problems" for the local authorities, according to police reports.

17. Her journal entry for July 15: "Passionate lovemaking with S. on the beach south of the cottage."

18. Following the supposed method of Gertrude Stein, the author began "encoding" certain aspects of her sexual life. Scholars note the surfeit of references to flowers, pistils, and stamens (often, perhaps humorously, *sous rature*), and to being "pollen-drunk." Her shopping lists become increasingly more obtuse and — to her redactors — intriguing during this period.

19. Marginalia: "No, no, no, no, no! This will not do!" Handwriting experts have long maintained that these comments are in the handwriting of the mysterious S. Biographers continue to insist that S. was simply a dramatic enactment of the author's "divided self."

20. Her journal entry for August 3: "Martinis on the Hotel Continental lawn with S. Long conversation about her childhood, so alien to my own. I was struck at how different a person I might be had I grown up in Haiti."

21. Increasingly, the author refers to the prejudice she felt growing up poor and black on the Lower East Side of Manhattan. Biographers, citing her rural Maine upbringing, believe these entries show the onset of her depression and a gradual descent into the delusional world that provoked the still-controversial "incident" two years later aboard the S.S. *Sunstruck,* when the ship foundered in shark-infested waters off the coast of Mexico.

22. She seems to be intimating a plan to kill herself here, though details are carefully coded.

23. "No flowers today from housekeeping" is thought to be a reference to her celibacy. A journal entry from the same time: "S. is COOL to me now. She locks herself in her room at the hotel and PRETENDS NOT TO BE AT HOME. But I can HEAR HER IN THEIR [*sic*] WALKING!" (Scholars note the strange grammatical error, the first of a series of uncharacteristic mistakes that would eventually overwhelm her writing and destroy her communicative abilities.)

24. Even as events in the "real world" became increasingly troubling for the author, she continued to wax theoretical about the disconnect between language and world: "It is not," she claimed in "Philosophical Assay #85," "S.'s lack of affection for me that causes me such pain, but the language by which I mediate that effect." Again, in #87, she states, "Pain is a linguistic phenomenon. I feel 'pain' in large part because I have a word for it."

25. In this section, the author's abilities with language are eroding, yet most commentators feel that this is the most powerful passage in the entire opus. Harold Broom of Manchester University has written in *Witness to an Execution: Last Poems of Madeleine du Plessix* that du Plessix's "gradual disintegration" is an emblem for "the artist's unquenchable thirst for both language and reality, a doubling that results in a terminally divided self. The demands of du Plessix's two masters are incommensurate and result in the destruction of the author herself. This is the pure language of pain—unintelligible, senseless, and despite itself, ruthlessly delightful."

26. The several references to Prospero in this final section are most often taken as codified foreshadowings of the author's undoing.

27. Here du Plessix echoes Paul de Man's famous statement that "death is a displaced name for a linguistic predicament." Perhaps a more appropriate quotation, found in one of her unsent letters to S., comes from Michel Foucault: "death is power's limit, the moment that escapes it."

28. "Sea, rise up and mete [meet?]. Torn water's mouth. / Heavy with paine, I sink. Sank." The measure is vague, the writing dissolute, but the meaning is clear and ominous. The bilingual pun on "Sank" (*Cinque*) remains a chilling final note: Madelcinc du Plessix apparently cast herself into the Gulf of Mexico's shark-infested waters from the tail fin of the S.S. *Sunstruck* on September 5.

Joy poured off the jade Buddha like water off a boulder in a high mountain stream, sunlight inside that water—all of it like a lit room at night. Where was it coming from? The jade Buddha, his sack slung on a stick, his belly big and full. High cholesterol. No attachments. Where was the happiness coming from? Put there by some Chinese prisoner? Where capital reached through the bars and gripped him by the back of his prison garment? Saying the Americans need jade Buddhas, saying carve some *nonattachment* in here, along the mouth. Carve some joy. While the caul of capital enclosed him, fixing him there, victim, the Buddha might say, of his own desires. Carve some *joyful-nonattachment* in there for our American friends. Carve some *toothless*. Carve some *feckless*. Carve some *no-mortgage* in there, some *no-car-payments* in there, too. Carve in some *no-college-loans*. Carve some *no-stock-market-fluctuations* in there where the belly swells; carve some *walking-carefree-in-the-flush-of-the-brow-caressing-moment*. Carve some *no-attachment-to-outcomes*, some *one-step-then-another*, *big-smile-with-no-teeth-in-it*. For our American friends. So they can glance as they attach themselves like trout to the *fly-with-mouth-sting-inside-it*, the *hunger-that-becomes-a-thrashing*. And the prisoner bowed and bent to his task.

MOON, PREDAWN COURTYARD, SANTA FE, NEW MEXICO

Unveiled now, the moon. Unburnished. And the clouds have given up their gold response. The bleached moon floats — unbattered by this earthly wind, the steady breath of the sun, huffing from the east, shaking all the leaves — and takes one last look into the predawn courtyard. Full moon, we say, as if it weren't always full. Full moon, its fullness determined by its position in relation to us, brief inhabitants of Earth, inventors, each moment, of time.

Like the moon, I woke from dreams I could not remember, though the vague shape of event was on me, in me — and the webs of passage. I sit now in this darkness. Darkness, and the wind, like hope itself, waking the leaves, scouring the dry grasses. Birdcalls, pop of gravel, crisping of tires in dirt, a single star in the Southwestern sky. Then car lights, the steady thrum and direction. The driver, secure in his purpose. Birdcalls rising now everywhere like flames on the brightening land.

Flower of abundance, the sexual flower, flower of horses galloping in a meadow, flower of criminal liability, flower of neglect and eventual triumph, flower of the archaic dream, the long-stemmed flower, flower of perfumed neck, flower that sprouts between the legs, the melting flower, flower of screaming in the night, the thick-stemmed flower, flower with its head under the pillow saying *no no no,* flower of girlhood, of leave-taking, risk-taking, flower rocking in the evening breeze, flower of walking alone under stars, moonflower, flower of humming-birds with jeweled throats, flower of car crash, of motorcycle skidding along the highway, of cancer opening like a hand, flower of midnight dog howl and the click of nails, houndstooth, dog lily, the flower of left lonely, flower of abandonment, flower of the sad fathers, flower of cold fact, the flower of the strummed guitar, toppled drumkit, flower of overwhelmed mother, flower of mystery, the life-giving and opulent flower, flower of walking hand in hand on the break-water, flower called girl-on-horseback, the loveliest flower, for you, the flower called horse-fallen, the yellow iris called horse-risen-to-gallop-again.

THE HORSE, SUSAN SAID

The horse, Susan said, because it is the blankest of slates, or because our successes are linked, has been written on extensively by our needs. Dumb giants pawing the ground, father, mother, escape, sexuality glistening and rippling, forelock and fetlock, footloose and fearless, or the pleasures of the fearful — fleeing the sudden gesture, careering through the green meadow at some imagined threat — shadow or shadow of a shadow, mirror glint — a world made meaningful by the creature's vulnerability, all the seams of that world, all the shifting angles. In here the cargo of a self; out there the quick and predatory gods inhabiting cliff top and meadow edge, lurking in arroyo and sinkhole, slinking along the rooftop. The world's mouth, ready to rend the flesh, to devour us. And sometimes, the pain in the fetlock seems to be coming from outside and the horse tries to outrun it. Isn't this the lesson the Buddha tries to teach us? We in our horse natures, galloping on, Susan said, galloping on.

Given that the universe will expand forever. Given that uncertainty plagues the equations. That the children dying are not our children. Given that we have tied both of our opponent's hands behind his back. Given the failures of diplomacy, blue cigar smoke, the muezzins and guzzlers, the catastrophic strophes of our peace-loving poets. Given the long walk back. Given tarmac. The seven levels of ambiguity. Given the crutch and the blade, the patriotic marches, yellow ribbons, quantum leaps, the blind followers of whom. Given the customary syntax. Given shock and awe, bunker buster, Humvee. Embedded journalists. Cell phone cameras. Given Black Hawk and stealth jet. Apaches in the sky. Given twenty-point bold. Given that each target is lit and the bonus points for that. Given oil-field fires, sacked museums. Given the tablets lugged through the blasted streets. Given the RAM, Pentium chip, night-vision goggles, and chemical suits. Given the training, conditioning, the time on our hands. Given the rations, the fuel, the window of op. Given that the citizens are busy elsewhere. Given the funky dance and twangy guitar. Given RVs, TVs, CDs, DVDs. Given the sitcom laughtrack. Given the tax cut. The six-foot screen. Given the full belly and a full slate of games. Given CNN. Given Fox. Given this day our daily bread, what else, Lord, would you have us do?

They couldn't decide if it *was* music — this merest tinkling and screeching — or hard wind scraping branches along a window in the night. Or if what the wind was doing — if, indeed, it was the wind — was music anyway. Someone said we would all die, the sun collapse, the earth hurled from its orbit, and what then of human music? Another insisted the music was already out there, the infinitesimal croonings and keenings swirling among red giants and dwarfs, swaddling Aldebaran and Polaris. And Rilke, of course, said music was our task — the music of naming. In this, he echoed Heidegger, whose presence befuddled and then angered Paul Celan, who made a music they would understand on Aldebaran if there were creatures who could live in that heat. Especially if there were such creatures. Then there was the matter of the human music of coupling, heartened and mimicked by the electric guitars yowling now from Bill's docked iPod. Bill was dating a writer now, a novelist, and the pain in his shoulders had relented enough that he could hoist his Stratocaster and resume the hammering and bending — those expressions of anguish that, though juvenile in conception, are adult in their execution and therefore, as the cries are purified in the crucible of technique, gain sophistication and emerge like adult lovemaking rather than the clunk and blather of teen humping. That a guitar could reveal so much. That the dancers gathered on the dance floor between scattered chairs and the unplugged jukebox would want to flail and sweat while others marveled or critiqued...I guess this is a prayer to the unsettled arc of mortality, the hoist and shuffle of this uncertain moment, our lives like bulbs flaring and going out as this city's seven million souls — ah, but that's another argument — click out their bedside lamps and curl toward whatever approximation of warmth they have found, while the music plays on in the streets below, the neon humming, the ambulances wailing the sudden shocked song of the living.

III

The world, it seems, is made up of wounders and the wounded,
and nobody, it seems, can tell the difference. And no one can say
why the guitar in its electrified moments wants to sound like an argument.

In a motel, in a going-home Buick, in a bar, even
in a ten-items-or-fewer line at Food Town. The world is will and idea,
said Schopenhauer, but the genius is without will. The genius

has knowledge, apparently, the way a skunk has stink.
Schopenhauer, himself a skunk of sorts, was shoved
down the stairs by his mother, a novelist who had never heard

of a family with two geniuses and meant to take care of that
inconsistency. But consistency, we would later learn,
is the hobgoblin of little minds. As in *never mind* or *mind your own business*

or *out of your mind.* Schopenhauer never played the electric guitar—
most likely, scholars suggest, because it had not yet been invented.
"I'd jump in the river but the water's too cold!" he might have sung

but that was sung by "The Hillbilly Shakespeare," whose guitar, though
sometimes amplified, was not, strictly speaking, electric.
It was among his many jokes about misery,

and means, according to the exegetes, that misery by itself,
that hamster that won't stop its incessant jogging in the exercise wheel
of our late night minds, is too rational, and has its own comforts

such that—and here's where we leave the exegetes, themselves far too rational.
Because what he meant to say is *I'd rather die asleep and far too drunk
in the back of a New Year's Oldsmobile on the way to a gig.* And so

he did. And Schopenhauer died garroted by inattention,
the pages of his most famous book used as bedding
in the beef slaughterhouse. Earlier, it had been fashionable

to name one's dog Immanuel Kant. A burgher, throwing open
a kitchen window at dawn, might call "Immanuel!" and twenty
yapping dogs would lope along the stone-paved streets.

Another burgher, interrupted in her reading of Goethe, might
fling open her second-floor shutter and toss a panful of hot water
dogward, cursing in a guttural German. Ah, the genealogy of morals,

the age of reason, the territorial imperative meeting the categorical imperative
on the streets of this small village at dawn! All this before the magistrates
could assemble their magisterial regalia. The dogs deciding everything

the way a horse decides to charge through the cholla then dance
like a stickered voodoo doll back to the barn. The way the coyotes yank
at the six corners of the jackrabbit and then give up, unable to cooperate

enough to finish eating the good meat. In my favorite version
of the year 2000, we were to wear huge exoskeletons and carry
2,000 pounds of whatever needed carrying easily on our backs.

But here we are, standing with thirteen items in the ten-items-or-fewer line.
Here we are with our electrified guitars. Some of us wounding;
some of us wounded. All of us singing about it. It's no wonder

we're confused. Our endoskeletons sag with the weight of our purchases
and we converse in a troubling language in which *bound*
means both *incapable of moving* and *moving at incredible speed*.

So in one version the man who was *bound to lose*
was unable to take a step; in another version, he could not stop himself.

TUBA CITY

after Richard Hugo

Dogs that no one owns run wise past ghosts
that no one sees. In the grocery your people fill
their carts with pop, with sacks of flour.
You drifted into town, half tanked

and mesmerized by two-lane roads. No hope.
The token white behind the register trails
dust with every step. His mother's house
is legend, so strewn with artifacts —

kachinas, turquoise, flat-style paintings —
that dust can't find the floor. No wall's
too full to host another local deity. The trading
post is thick with tourists up from Flag, their hands,

like finches, skitter in the trinkets. That
high school is divided blue for Hopi, green
for Navajo — those borders white men made.
Aging hippies cruise the fair so luckless

they grow hair sideways and top it with berets.
They festoon their foppishness with beads.
The high school English teacher, Mrs. Fink
from Terre Haute, drives a Falcon full of books.

She deems the honor students "braves"
and billboards words like *cavalier*
and *crux*. Her smile's bright and dry as Phoenix
in July. All week it's fry bread, beans, a jug of lemonade.

On market day, the Hopis drag you out for barbecue.
Stone to adobe—dust is thick as history here.
HUD homes. Signs that say *Get Sober,*
Stay. In the hostel smiling Christians strum

guitars and sing till 2 a.m. When the knocking comes,
that wistful blonde, sixteen and Bible heavy,
smiles so sweet you take the book. A window
prop. The Navajo you shot hoops with

behind the Hopi school took his game to Page,
where whites don't mind his tongue can't shape
the fricatives and glottal stops, can't form the word
for enemy. And everywhere the wire fences hum

some song they sing up there, beyond the town.
The language strange, they say *past* for *happiness,*
begin for *keeping on.* You say *drought* and mean
that dogs are wise and ghosts can't find the pathway home.

THE POT SPINNERS

for Briana

*In the literature the tribe is known as the Pot Spinners, but
that was the name given them by their neighbors to the east.
They called themselves the People.*

They lived where the light plunged into the mountains — at that point of
    exhaustion.

The cross-hatching indicated north, where moss would gather, where the mud
    wall would crumble and the wood slowly rot, where the snow lay late
    into May.

When the former partners removed their last belongings, the camp was
    darkened by new shadows.

New shadows on the stone fire ring, new shadows across the mud hut, new
    shadows scuffling on the red dirt pathway.

Two quick vertical strokes indicated where they entered the story.

Betrayal. New affections. One name removed. Then both.

Untaking this man.

Untaking this woman.

Acres of cholla were a kind of menace, a limit.

The path out had to circle the hazards.

The man waving the stone ax over his head was, according to the code,
    justified, but nothing would be accomplished.

The man bounding over the cholla was an emblem for what?

Years later, when the image started appearing on the tribe's pottery, it was a
    comic image.

The man's hair depicted as a lightning field.

His spread legs clearing the cholla's spikes were bent impossibly, his arms
    uplifted as though something were shocking him.

There was always a small bird on one shoulder, but no one could say what
    that meant.

He would clear the cholla, but not by much.

A single thorn in one calf suggested that he would escape but not entirely.

The humor arose half in the depiction and half in the fact that he was depicted
        at all.

That he had become an emblem. That the tribe wanted the emblem.

That the story was worth repeating.

At first, archaeologists considered the clans pictured along the bottom of the
        pots a design element.

If you spin a pot in your hands you can see that they are crying first then
        laughing then crying again.

Nobody, the legend says, once he has begun to spin the pot, can stop.

1

Click-click, door-squeal, chair-scrape.
Fuckfuckfuck in the darkened kitchen.

The child pulls the blankets tight,
watches the bright light framing the door.

Then the mother's whisper, the father's growling slur.

Then *Stop it. Stop. It.*
The snickering of the—

Then the six-year-old launching his head into the father's stomach,
eyes squeezed shut, fists thrashing,
the dark theater of his head sizzling and bursting with light.

Formica table, sugar bowl, spoon, blue flame,
quickening gurgle of a coffeepot.

2

When the camera pans the still landscape—meadow turning golden in dawn-
    light, stone wall, five crows ruffling and preening in the branch tops,
    the riven oakbark—we anticipate the crash.

When in the midst of the crash—the glass shattering, metal collapsing,
    tearing, hands thrown up for protection, the head snapping on its thin
    stalk—we anticipate the silence after.

In the silence after, we await a sign—head turning, hand reaching, a beginning.

They all wanted something to happen and when it did they wanted it to stop.

When it stopped, they wanted it to happen again.

So when the man walks out of the detox unit to meet his ex-wife in the coffee
      shop, it is the bear sleeping in the cave of his stomach that keeps
      her talking.

That the bear is there, that she knows it, that it promises to make the good
      days shimmer.

FESTIVAL OF NATURAL DISASTERS

1. ATTRACTIONS

The willows tossed their heads like supermodels in a group shot.
All the preening was prolegomena. Encomium.
The main event was an anaerobic gasping in the yews.
We were modern, after all, and mimicked the latest walk.
Above us, the Art People circulated in their cubicles.
Above us, the athletic and starved-for-fashion.
All the looking was prepared for by a brief speech.
If our gazes fell on the rump, a certain number of points were earned.
On the legs, a different number.
The score was kept secretly, by the Director of Aesthetics.
A clerk of sorts with his handheld counter.
Meanwhile, huge flocks of blackbirds kept demonstrating the latest theories
   above the nuclear marsh.
Adamant tourists were carting their cameras and water bottles to the marsh
   edge.
Unbeknownst to the Chamber, they were scuffling in the sphagnum, looking
   for the attractions.
They adjusted their visors, leveled their optics.
Were the blackbirds the attraction?
The sullen towers and baffling switchyards?
The voluptuous willows? The supermodels?
Where were the attractions?
And why the furtive gasping and wheezing in the shrubbery?

2. PROSPECTUS

Attendance at the annual Festival of Natural Disasters continues to climb.
Despite the incursions of lava and the subsequent fires.
Despite the earthquake-addled gazebo.

A British economist, in a recent study, has charted the growth of per capita
dollars made available in a "disaster tourist" economy.

Admitting, of course, that there are fewer capitae.

In the upcoming movie version, the mayor will be played by Harvey
Gorpmann, best known for his portrayal of Little Hal in the TV
docudrama *Born in a Men's Room, Raised in a Closet, Fed Dogfood by His
Schoolteacher Parents.*

Protestors, concerned over this casting, have gathered in a designated area
along the fault line.

Tourists may regard this quaint but constitutionally protected protest through
the telescopes provided at the gazebo.

Though the great distance renders the placards indecipherable, tourists are
invited to invent possible slogans.

The most imaginative will be printed in the *Natural Disaster News,* distributed
free at retail outlets throughout the region.

3. NATURAL DISASTERS

Gasping and wheezing.

And the permanence in the structures, running along the seams.

And the permanence where they were making the sentences.

The men had decided to wear powdered wigs; the women cinched their waists
with the leather they softened with saliva.

There were lawyers to advise and make more incomprehensible laws, which
required more advice.

Under the gazebo's flimsy roof, the townsfolk gathered to watch the funnel
clouds and share in child care.

An unprecedented genius caused the children's heads to glow.

The tourists consulted their brochures, checked their watches.

It was the hour when everything was inoculated against desire.

It was the hour when the language encircling the photographs met the sun
setting over the reservoir and created the unexpected but hoped-for
congruence.

"Oh, hallelujah," they cried. "We are finally getting our money's worth."

And a brass band marched through the gladioli, honking a new, improved
    anthem.

The mayor appeared briefly and coughed into her fist.

Everyone cheered and held his or her complimentary long-stemmed rose
    skyward.

Gratitude fluttered over the crowd like a flock of swallows.

In photographs of the event, now on sale at the historical society, a vague
    nostalgia has already settled over the mayor's face.

She seems perpetually about to speak, though there is no record of her having
    spoken.

Later, the survivors lamented the insufficiently bulwarked dam, the poor
    placement of the village.

Others cited the volcano building itself in Terwilliger's fields.

Inside his head, the fragments collude:
river of metal, river of sheen, eyes of a woman
gone muddy like a southern river — flickering
like time, all cohesion gone, ministering now
to the chaos. The relief between foldings,
infoldings, where nuance meets grand scheme.
Inside his head, where ends call out to causes,
where dreams drive him downward first,
into the subtonic, the slithering bass line,
where misery tilts its porkpie and strides
blithely down the October street of vendors
with their fenced merchandise, their knockoff
watches and CDs lined on the sidewalk.
Then the bridge, quick modulation, then the solo,
all technique where the fingers meet the keys,
all life-falling-apart in the chest. A wail
at the edge of musicality, sweetness,
lover on your chest, all *moment,* all *now*
with the light dying across the Hudson,
dying, yes, but all *now,* you could see it that way,
all *now,* the smell of her hair, her eyes
big and hopeful, all *now,* then the sudden snarl
of everything waiting, the sirens flaring below,
the lights coming on against dusk,
all the denials waking in the veins,
in the nerves, the solo shrieking *now,*
baby in pain and the chords keep changing
keep churning underneath *now*
he's grappled his truck to the pillars *now*

he's revving the engine dropping the clutch
now he's tearing it all down angry child because
he can't have everything all the time forever—

THE IMMORTALS

for John Langdon

That they have sidestepped death makes them powerful.
That each day is thick with opportunity.
That this one takes guitar lessons, that one paints landscapes.
Another is sculpting her abs in the gym.

Most days, they avoid reminiscing.
Most days they spend perfecting a minor art.
They lunch on a salad of gratitude and bliss.
Dine early. Sleep soundly.

But sometimes, before dawn, an image from the past flares —
betrayal, death of a child, twisted metal, sirens.
Something somebody said that was hurtful.
Something they thought was theirs taken away.

And sadness flames up from somewhere in the chest.
And burns there, fading and flaring, almost unbearable.
Until the earth tilts.
Until sunlight brings color to roses, and birds begin to stir.

And they are called once again to their activities and appointments.
Their duties, distractions.
And the sadness fades, leaving them efficient and eager and prompt.

WHAT NOW?

after Thelonious Monk

And Monk wiring the bridge with
little explosions, a handful of nails tossed
just to see what will happen —
the wobble and swerve, the screech,
the sweetness undercut by the grieving piano,
grieving because the world requires grieving
and celebration, requires — when the car
went over, when the fire stuck its tongue
out the apartment window, when the child
dreamed in her makeshift crib of summertime,
sleeping on the beach, and the heat, when
the wheels kept spinning in the night
and the radio played its summer party song
to the splinters of glass, the buckled steel —
it was Monk who knew Monk who knew
Monk who knew Monk who knew
in singing not to sing who knew to slap
just ahead or behind, who knew this swing
this life this beautiful falseness was too much
and then — what now? — hand hovering
like a hawk over Fifth Ave., the stoop,
plunge and grab, the lingering burst of feathers.

In the drowse of the saxophone, in that bittersweet drama, roses on the
        nightstand, one shoulder bared.
Summer evenings, warm pavement underfoot, she would slip her hand into
        his pocket and jingle his change.
"What is love?" the "soulful" chanteuse sang, "flowers and champagne /
        a walk in the lane / oh, baby, ain't that love?"
When the narrative fractured, the vermilion sky darkened.
The alto was given to sweetness, but ideas about sweetness launched flights of
        discordant squawking.
The papers called this "The Modern Condition."
A certain motif presented itself and they all joined in.
The light changed and a ruckus ensued — Subarus, Porsches, Fleetsides,
        Stepsides, earnest bicyclists wobbling among the drainage and litter.
The lovers imagined the traffic noise was a waterfall.
The lovers imagined a great affection circulating along the greenbelt, among
        the placid waterfowl, the stream "coursing" through these natural
        settings.
That they were exempt from suffering was itself a kind of suffering.
The stockbrokers and magistrates, the mannered speeches and posturing
        glam-rockers; the cheerful and the winded; the sunset smearing its
        orange sentiments across the New England horizon.
Even the homeless have the flamboyance of rock stars   their assembled rags,
        hopeful speeches, the artful presentation of their desires.
Then the string quartet in the gazebo, a pleasant falseness they longed for
        when the muttering ducks surrounded them, their hungers upon them
        like the polyblend uniforms of the doomed.
Later, there would be frozen yogurt, light caresses, laughter, plotless fiction,
        ubiquitous music.

1. A SUFFICIENCY

In the pristine dawn, dawn of possibility, dawn of cat-crying-in-the-hemlock,
dawn of turkeys-across-the-valley, dawn of hummingbird-buzz-and-
chitter, a man tries to remember how this was once enough.
Grass passing under his feet, the frost-tipped grass, wind across his bare legs,
cardinal's insistent *keer, keer* from the forsythia, jays raucous on their
marauding flights.
Enough. Sufficient. Hours in the tree fort, whole afternoons by the stream.
And then fear flushed him from the high grass?
And the interstate starting up, and the coyotes' last shivering howls before sleep.
Dogs swaying in the grip of their fidelities, settling back into their grassy beds.

Where to go from here?
Into the darkness, child. Darkness of oblivions. Of worry and disharmony. Of
chatter by the watercooler. Airports and cell phones. Scotch and soda.
The comforting prison of a schedule.
Into the light, child. Light that whitens every page. That illuminates the
daily chores.

2. A BASKET FULL OF HEADS

When the chants rise over the mountains.
When the birds sing out from the hollows in their bones.
When the traffic's hum and howl call him out from the canticle of his dreams
(the dog rollicking across suburban lawns, the woman whose voice
kept changing her into a series of surprising women from his
past) — how will he answer?
The children gather and wait.
Why has he made himself so important?
And yet never quite here, never quite now.

Always the quick glimpse at the place where he expects the future to arrive,
   lumbering giant with a basket full of heads.
His among them.

   3. INSIDE THE FIRE

At first they could not they could not and then they had.

It was an old story—a handful of bees and they could not uncup their hands.

That they wanted to be both inside each other and outside circumstance.

The aspen grove shimmered in autumn light and wind.

The waves the particles were building a shimmering in the aspens.

The descriptions were fluttering all along the pathways.

Then, the mirror which depicted him entering her her being entered or in some
   ideologies her dissolving him in the solvent of her self.

Man : woman as this river rock : that river rock.

And the almost inaudible clacking.

Inside, the fire.

And inside the fire, the destinations.

Havoc was the name of the party hat they'd chosen for the occasion.

So when the raven rolled upside down.

When the moon grew "fat and sullen."

When the train screeched and squealed and rumbled through the midnight
   town.

When the leftover adobes swelled with rain and the children's fort became
   mounds of earth.

And the sirens indicated a tragic arrival.

And the numinous fell like gauze over the man leaned against the pickup
   filled with melons and squash.

And the woman's rise and fall, firelight flickering over her face her hair,
   sculpting her breasts, and the man facing the fire, his eyes two engines
   of praise.

Together, on Earth, in this paradise of kissing and looking, the perpetual
   entering and being entered.

And the tawny flycatcher sculling under the portal.

Picking delicately the newly hatched spiders from the web.

Where the dusk-light rested against the skylight like a coat of gesso.

Outside, the wings' softnesses, the feathered, the downy, the delicate and
      light-soaked plumage.

Inside, the tenderness of her nape, his hand just now touching, stroking the
      wisps of hair, the tendoned and muscled, the mortal neck.

4. A CONGRUENT SONG

Like grapefruit on market day, when the vendors make themselves exemplary,
      when they wear the clothing of the pristine past we keep trying to deny.

When their hands make change from cloth aprons.

When they call us into the circle of their mock gratitude.

When they make of their fruits and vegetables an altar to purity.

And the earth tumbles through black space.

And the tribes gather their weapons.

And the perpetual slaughter begins again.

But these peaches, so lovely in the morning sunlight.

He presses his face near them. Breathes in "the bounty of earth's delights."

Now. Just peach-smell. Now. Sunlight on his head.

Now. Three or four flies. Their buzzing flights.

Just this. Peaches that smell like peaches.

And the goldfinches in the Russian elms sing a congruent song.

And the finches in the ivy chatter a congruent song.

And the woman playing with the change in her apron hums a congruent song.

And each head in the basket like a grapefruit on market day.

When the midnight phone rang,
my friend's voice kept trying
to say the word *hysterectomy,* that
one-word melody with ancestors
stalking the madhouses of nineteenth-
century England. I was, of course,
moved, more by the simple
failure of elocution than the illness —
which was a factoid in a slick
magazine. Like learning that a giraffe
has seven neck bones, that a bat
will eat a ton of mosquitoes
in an average year. Hysterectomy.
Abstract as a memo from the President
of Nocturnal Congestion. The dishes
shifted in their dishwater nest. The refrigerator
hummed its cryogenic folksongs.
The budgerigar honked and chittered
in its night-shrouded cage. I wrapped
the phone cord around my finger
like a man wrapping a phone cord
around his finger. The voice
in the telephone. The voice in
the telephone. I kept hearing
appendectomy, lobotomy, laparoscopy.
The sadness soaking into the words
like hand cream. The words thick with it,
bloated. Seven neck bones. Imagine.
Like you. Like me. But the miraculous reach.

UTILITARIANISM

for Grayce

Salisbury morning stippled with flowers—
azaleas flaring by the door, rhododendrons
sporting their red boutonnieres, magnolias
like huge pink artichokes. And birdsong—
lisping warblers in the linwoods, the flicker's
ratcheting call, mockingbird on the chimney
auctioning the moment. I tried to steer her,
just three years old, past the robin.
Expert at noticing, she walked straight to it.
"What happened to his head," she asked.
"Hit by a car," I said. She looked and looked,
put hands on her knees as she leaned in
to study the grizzled ruff of feathers, ants
climbing the bent beak, diving into the eye sockets.
Finally, she straightened. "Oh, well," she said
—around us birdsong brilliant and the blossoming world—
"all the others birds   have their heads."

PIÑON & MOON

for Teresa

Dawn. And the full moon sank like milky quartz through quilted clouds,
sank toward the mesa where he'd found the bull snake skin curled around
       the juniper,
sank until it lit up the belly of the piñon tree on the ridgetop. *That is how
I feel,* he thought, the secret blazing inside him, glowing. He thought
We must be radiant; this knowledge must make us radiant. The planet
was just awakening — the rooster across the valley was making its
first ragged calls, the finches were finding each other with their tentative
questions (*here? here?*), and his own species was traveling the highways
and rails (a single jet crossing the eastern sky), fleeing or gathering in cities.
He'd been thinking of her and reading *Human Wishes,* thinking
that what he wanted from poetry was a species of rigorous tenderness,
unsentimental, maybe even brutal. Brutal in its failures — the attempted
(the fumbled) touching and the long aftermath of gazing. Gazing
through windows, for example, at the rain falling though a peach tree,
at what he thought of as "the rain's steady questioning." She had worked
a wedding across town, under the full moon, a moon, she'd said
when she'd called him on her cell phone from outside the kitchen,
that was making everyone drink excessively and act — she couldn't say
exactly how they were acting except to say they seemed like
they were "waiting for something to happen." He was in love with her
and envious of anyone who got to watch her moving through
the moon-soaked night carrying her tray of nori rolls and so
the "waiting" had an air of ominousness. She would dance later,
and because she gave herself to every task the way California soil
gives itself to sliding in the rainy season, he knew the men
would lose their way inside that dancing, as he had. It was what he loved —
the quick passions that lit in her eyes, her face a flight of finches

whirling over a misty field, in Vermont, say, a summer morning
when the first child out of bed is carrying a fishing pole resolutely
down the dirt road. Her hair, reddening in the dawn-light, is pulled
to one side. The summer sun has spattered new freckles across her nose.
One quarter of a century will pass before he finds her, but it has
already begun. He walks beside her on the road, walks quietly.
He doesn't want her to forget him, doesn't want her to notice him.
The moon falling now, behind the mesa, elicits an unexpected peace.
Does the piñon tree swallow the moon or does the moon enter the piñon?
The ravens drift over the valley in raucous first flight. Later, he knows,
when he meets her for coffee, he will be ravished by her presence,
and when the cool breeze rises, they will close their eyes together
as it touches first her skin, because she sits to the west, and then his.

Silence in this suburb of cars and dogs, of roar
and rumble, sudden thump at the railroad crossing.
But this morning before 5:00 a.m., there's only the wash,
the waterfall of cars on I-25, which sounds in my ear
almost like the sound of blood in my arteries —
that inner traffic. In the predawn silence
a bright crescent of moon, darkness visible,
the flared edge. Now a dog barks. Now a single bird.
Another. Now a car in the distance. Dog. Bird,
farther off, this time. Just this one moment of silence
before the traffic begins, before the full choir of dogs
and birds and coyotes flush with desire, as I begin,
shaken and shaking now in the lee of in the wake of
in the grip of what unnameable fierce beauty.

LOVING HORSES

for Grayce

Yellow aspen. Quaking leaf. Metal barn creaking.
Dust like rain against the roof. What could be better
than a horse dreaming in a sunlit stall? The heave
of chest, the nostrils flaring. The head carving light
into shadow and deeper shadow. The sheen of a horse's coat
is a form of weeping, the form weeping takes
when it hears the solitary cry of the flicker
in the fog-softened morning. The cry of the flicker
which is the word *tear* lengthened and brought to bear
upon the meadow's longings, the longings we bring to the meadow.
Which are the same longings we bring to the horse in the dawn.
The eye seems bottomless. Fetlock and pastern seem designed
more for flight than galloping, tendons taut as the bones
in a bat's wing. The bats which veer across the barn's mouth
in the dusk, feeding on the flies which feed on the horses
which feed on the hay scattered in their outdoor runs.
Yellow aspen. Quaking leaf. Metal barn creaking.
Dust like rain against the roof. What could be better than a horse
galloping with horses in a rain-freshened meadow?
The young women lean and listen to the soliloquy of hoofbeats.
In a gallop, as we first saw in Muybridge's photographs,
all four hooves are off the ground at once. *Walk.*
Working trot. Extended trot. Canter. Gallop.
Count strides to the fence. Fold. Take the fence.
Sit up. Gallop on. It is thought that the horse,
because it cannot see immediately ahead,
must remember the jump it jumps blindly, guided by the rider's
hands and seat and legs. And the rider must look past the jump,

head up, to keep the horse's energy moving forward
so that of the three — horse, rider, spectator — only the spectator sees
the actual jump as it is jumped. Which is a metaphor for life,
the way this moment I am in, this moment I am trying to be in,
does not exist until I am in the next one. The *nextness* of the fences —
the way a man who is leaving his wife for another woman
can no longer see the wife he is leaving. Or the way the child struggles
with the piano concerto until she begins to work
on the next, more difficult, concerto which makes the first one
easy to play and filled with something like joy
where before there was only agony. Which reminds me of an afternoon —
it was the son's birthday, and the mother invited the father
to a party at the house she lived in with her new lover. The father
brought his current lover who spent the afternoon measuring
the distance between herself and the ex-wife, between the father
and the wife's new lover. These were fences that needed jumping
at a full gallop, and she could only see them
when she turned her head to one side and then, when she
needed to jump, they would have already disappeared. *Dad,*
my daughter might say if she were watching over my shoulder.
Why do you turn everything into a lecture? The poem
is about horses and horses are about themselves.
Yellow aspen. Quaking leaf. Metal barn creaking.
Dust like rain against the roof. The horses stomp and sway, shift their weight
from leg to leg. *So handsome,* my daughter says. We are sitting in my Jeep,
leaving the barn on an afternoon on which I'd struggled,
in a counseling session, to explain how I had tried
desperately not to fall in love with the woman
I had already fallen in love with. It is late afternoon, the sun is setting
magnanimously over the Jemez Mountains, and her horse, Codeman —
half muscular Hanoverian, half elegant Thoroughbred — has come out
to dip his light-sculpting head into the water trough. *Look at him, Dad.*
Her voice is hushed, almost a whisper. *Just   look at him*

MA ROULOTTE

fresh leaves, two dark lilac-coloured irises and
a mass of orange or sulphur-yellow marigolds

PIERRE BONNARD

Not "pleasure," where pleasure expresses
its "evolutionary significance,"
where the tumble of sex
preserves the species, where
the genes cheer
from their orchestra seats.

But first sunlight
on the flowered bedspread.
A lover's handwriting among the unpaid bills.
The "weightlessness of birds."
A dream of prosperity.

Not pleasure as rehearsal for.
Not pleasure as drive.
Not accounts payable, accounts received.

But the journal of moments:
Fingers brushing cheek, nape,
sweeping and gathering.
One finger drawn
behind the ear, along the jaw.
Nerve-ends crackling,
skin waking, shivering.

Not words with their cords dangling.
Not words with their unspecifiable velocities,
their unsteady allegiances.

But lips and tongues and fingers — that actual
assent and lather. Affections gathering
in the air. The air
leaning over them. Behaviors
charging the molecules. Behaviors
swirling among the poplars,
lifting the birds, filling
each absence with meaning.

And form:
The form sunlight assumes
on the wooden sill, the red
stone floor, the plaster wall.
Clouds in a blue vase. Blue
vase in the sky.

Through *la porte ouverte:*
the billowing pleasure of flowers.

It was evolving into something else. Under the surface.

Inside, where the betrayals launched their unforeseen monsoons.

Where the monsoons swept over the rocky plain of fidelities.

There was something that needed to be said in a kind of code.

The code of paint on the coveralls. Blue in the palace of fiction.

Red in the tumbledown shack where they stacked the truth.

Fire in the alcove. Dying bats in the _____.

They had to choose the French pronunciation or be asked to leave.

And yet the Americanized word seemed inhabitable: Foyer.

They were in the *foyer* when they were discovered.

Slacks, they supposed, because they were roomy. And Rumi,

someone said, is a poet of the spirit *extraordinaire*. Ah, yes.

And the *bibliothèque* was on the right. Someone had to return

some books. In stilted French. Above them all, but tottering,

singing *Voulez-vous couchez avec moi:* The Mayor of Condolences glad-handing the misanthrope beside the cruise ship. When,

the exasperated reader wanted to know, will you get serious?

You were four years old. Your father was a midnight crashing, hoarse cough,

cataleptic on the davenport. Bottle of whiskey dug

up on the job. No money left. And no food. You were four, and

you recognized "the gravity of the situation." There was gravity

in the sugar bowl. Gravity pulled at the doilies. Gravity

wore its black boots all night, walking on the roof. Later,

nobody could be serious enough. Broken guitar. Some screaming.

Doors slammed. Screeching of tires. Dropped off, the bunch of you,

at the home of the man who stabbed one's elbow if one placed it

on the dinner table. But enough of that. In the cool morning

the tractor sounded clean. One could climb aboard and watch

the crisp world go past. Cows at the water hole; horses under the maple.

Light mist hovering over the greenest grass. The cool air blowing past.

Engine warming one's legs. The throttle opening like joy itself.

Did a dog run alongside? Nobody could say one didn't.

Did a rooster crow from a fencepost? In some versions one did.

Was the woman's name Mabel? Did she wear an apron?

Did she bring you fresh bread where you sat warming in the sun?

And when you plowed the deep furrows, did the soil turn

almost black in the morning light? The chickens running alongside

pecking at the cutworms and earthworms you turned up—

It's true you were all whipped when the model plane was smashed.

It's true you were all whipped when you giggled in the attic.

It's true you were a stranger everywhere you went.

But you turned up potatoes in the side yard. And on a crisp morning

you reached into the warmth underneath the setting hen

and slid out three fresh eggs, oval and brown and warm.

Jon Davis is the author of three chapbooks and three full-length collections of poetry. He has received numerous awards for his poetry, including a Lannan Literary Award, two National Endowment for the Arts Fellowships, and the Lavan Younger Poets Award from the Academy of American Poets. For the past twenty years, he has been a professor of creative writing at the Institute of American Indian Arts in Santa Fe, New Mexico.

The Chinese character for poetry is made up of two parts: "word" and "temple." It also serves as pressmark for Copper Canyon Press.

Since 1972, Copper Canyon Press has fostered the work of emerging, established, and world-renowned poets for an expanding audience. The Press thrives with the generous patronage of readers, writers, booksellers, librarians, teachers, students, and funders — everyone who shares the belief that poetry is vital to language and living.

Major funding has been provided by:

Amazon.com

Anonymous

Beroz Ferrell & The Point, LLC

Golden Lasso, LLC

Lannan Foundation

National Endowment for the Arts

Cynthia Lovelace Sears and Frank Buxton

Washington State Arts Commission

For information and catalogs:

COPPER CANYON PRESS
Post Office Box 271
Port Townsend, Washington 98368
360-385-4925
www.coppercanyonpress.org

This book is set in Baskerville 10, a digital reworking of the eighteenth-century English type of John Baskerville by František Štorm. Titles are set in Officina Sans designed by Erik Spiekermann. Book design and composition by Valerie Brewster, Scribe Typography. Printed on archival-quality paper at McNaughton & Gunn, Inc.